Understanding Cryptocurrencies

Ethereum and Its Applications

Disclaimer

The sole purpose of this book is to provide information. The information contained in this book is provided on an as is basis, and the author is not responsible for the accuracy of information provided in the book.

The content within this book has been derived from various sources. The reader should consult professionals before implementing any advice mentioned in the book. Under no circumstances will any blame or legal responsibility be held against the publisher, or author, for any damages, reparation, or monetary loss due to the information contained within this book.

Investing, cryptocurrency trading and gambling involves considerable risk of loss and is not suitable for every investor. The value of an asset may fluctuate, causing investors to lose more than their original investment. You should not engage in investing, cryptocurrency trading and gambling if you don't fully understand how the transactions work and if you don't understand your level of risk with each transaction.

Table of Contents

Introduction...1

Brief History of Ethereum 1

Release of The Ethereum Whitepaper 1

Ethereum Crowdfunding Campaign 2

Development Work, Events and Programs..2

Four Stages of Ethereum 3

DOA Attack 3

Formation of Ethereum Classic 4

Tangerine Whistle..5

Enterprise Ethereum Alliance..5

Metropolis..5

Ethereum – The "World Computer"..6

How Ethereum Works 7

The Transaction Diagram 7

Nodes 8

Full and Lightweight Nodes 8

Distribution of Ethereum Nodes..8

Consensus Protocol..9

The Mining Process 9

Nonce Value 9

Comparison b/w PoW and PoS...9

Mining Reward 10

Mining Difficulty..10

Ethash 10

ASIC Mining 10

Expansion in Capacity 10

Ethereum Wallets..10

Ether...11

Fuel for the Network..11

Ether Calculation 11

How to Buy Ether 11

Smart Contracts 12

Example 12

Smart Contract History 12

How Smart Contracts Work..13

Language for Smart Contracts 14

Anatomy of a Smart Contract 14

Are Smart Contracts Smart? 14

Are Smart Contracts Smart Legal Contracts?...14

Applications of Ethereum 15

20 Ethereum Use Cases 15

1. Status...15

2. MetaMask 15

3. Opera..15

4. Golem 16

5. Local Ethereum..16

6. Compound..16

7. Bounties Network 16

8. Ethlance 17

9. Minds 17

10. CryptoKitties..17

11. Dolomite DEX 17

12. IDEX...18

13. Uport...18

14. Augur 18

15. Ujo 19

16. Marble...19

17. MakerDAO 19

18. Gitcoin 20

19. Etheremon...20

20. Super Player..21

The Future of Ethereum..22

Challenges and Limitations 22

Scalability 22

Sharding...22

Hacking..23

Proof of Stake 23

Off-Chain Transactions 23

Leader 23

Ethereum 2.0..24

Phases 24

Economics...24

Migration 26

Introduction

Brief History of Ethereum

The introduction of Bitcoin created a new and existing space for developers. Suddenly, blockchain technology and cryptocurrencies became a much-discussed topic in the media. One of the people who was part of this developer community was co-founder of Bitcoin magazine, Vitalik Buterin. The Canadian teenager founded the magazine in 2011 at the age of 17. As a programmer, Vitalik was interested in the technical aspects of the blockchain. One of the things he noticed about blockchain projects was that each new project started from the creation of a new blockchain. This was something he thought could be changed about the emerging technology. Instead of everyone having to create their own blockchain, what if there was a blockchain that could allow people to build their applications on it? This improvement of the technology was one of the driving forces behind the creation of Ethereum.

"I thought [those in the Bitcoin community] weren't approaching the problem in the right way. I thought they were going after individual applications; they were trying to kind of explicitly support each [use case] in a sort of Swiss Army knife protocol," says Vitalik, according to a Forbes publication.

It's important to note here that Bitcoin and Ethereum have many similarities. Both blockchains have a decentralized network that can be used for anonymous transactions between accounts. The differences are that Bitcoin was made for currency transactions and the programming language doesn't enable people to use the Bitcoin blockchain in the same way they can with Ethereum (more on the Ethereum blockchain in the next section).

Release of The Ethereum Whitepaper

In 2013, Vitalik put his concepts on paper and published the Ethereum white paper, which is available on GitHub. The white paper details the purpose of Ethereum and how transactions will work on the Ethereum blockchain. The same year, they officially announced the project at the North American Bitcoin Conference in Florida with the following list of founders: Vitalik Buterin, Anthony Di Iorio, Charles Hoskinson, Mihai Alisie, & Amir Chetrit.

"The intent of Ethereum is to create an alternative protocol for building decentralized applications, providing a different set of trade-offs that we believe will be very useful for a large class of decentralized applications, with particular emphasis on situations where rapid development time, security for small and rarely used applications, and the ability of different applications to very efficiently interact, are important," according to the white paper.

To achieve this goal, Ethereum would focus its efforts on creating "a blockchain with a built-in Turing-complete programming language, allowing anyone to write smart contracts and decentralized applications where they can create their own arbitrary rules for ownership, transaction formats and state transition functions," mentions the white paper.

The design was built on the philosophy of simplicity, universality, modularity, agility, and non-discrimination, non-censorship. Simplicity means that that an average programmer can implement the code, and the language is simple even if it means that there is some time inefficiency and storage capacity inefficiency. Universality means the presence of an internal turning complete language that any programmer can use to create this smart contract or other mathematically definable transaction. Modulation means that the protocol is modular so modifications can be made easily when needed. Agility will allow connect modifications, such as scalability improvements, when needed. Non censorship and discrimination means that there shouldn't be any restrictions on how someone is using the network.

The next steps involved outlining the technical specification and funding of the project. The funding was preceded by the release of the Ethereum Yellow paper in early 2014. In the Yellow paper, Dr. Wood detailed the technical specifications for the Ethereum Virtual Machine (EVM) (discussed in detail later).

The specifications were used by clients to create several open source implementations of the Ethereum code in several programming languages including Go, Rust, C++, Python, Java, JavaScript, and Haskell. The most popular one of these implementations is in the Go language.

Ethereum Crowdfunding Campaign
To fund their ambitious new project, they turned to crowdsourcing. The cofounders, including two new co-founders Dr. Gavin Wood and Jeffrey Wilcke, launched a crowdsourcing campaign in 2014 and were able to raise over $180 million USD.

The crowdfunding involved the presale of the cryptocurrency, Ether. The crowd sale ran for the months of July and Aug 2014 and generated a sale of 11.9 million Ether tokens. The Ethereum team traded Ether with Bitcoin to pay the developers and legal fees.

The legal and financial complexities of a presale meant that the team needed to create several legal entities. In early 2014, the development of Ethereum was formalized through a Swiss company, Ethereum Switzerland GmbH (EthSuisse). After specifying the concept in the yellow paper, the team also created a Swiss non-profit foundation, the Ethereum Foundation (Stiftung Ethereum). After the ether presale, they created a non-for-profit organization called ETH DEV. The non-profit is headed by Vitalik Buterin, Gavin Wood, and Jeffrey Wilcke and it manages the development of Ethereum.

Development Work, Events and Programs
The ETH DEV team delivered several proof-of-concepts (POC) for evaluation by the community. In Nov 2014, developers organized the DEVCON-0. Held in Berlin, the five-day conference was attended by Ethereum developers from all around the world. The discussions and presentations at DEVcon-0 shed light on important initiatives for making the platform more reliable and scalable. The conference also discussed the overall vision of Ethereum and development of Dapps.

The following year, a DEVgrant programme was announced. According to the Ethereum Blog posting, the program "offers funding for contributions to both the Ethereum platform, and projects based on Ethereum. Its goals are threefold:

To provide developers interested in contributing to the Ethereum ecosystem the opportunity to spend significant time on their project, in order to bring it to completion.

To extend the codebase with useful components that are not the main focus of ΞTHDEV, but which would be very valuable to users of Ethereum generally.

To increase our outreach to other communities and the general public."

A security audit of Ethereum spanned from late 2014 to early 2015. Several proofs of concepts were released in 2014 and 2015, leading to Olympic, the 9th POC open testnet. Developers were invited to test the network and rewards were offered to those who found vulnerabilities.

Four Stages of Ethereum
The extended Ethereum launch consists of four stages: Frontier, Homestead, Metropolis (current phase) and Serenity.

Frontier

The first version of Ethereum was launched in July 2015. Called Frontier, this version provided the basic functionality for the platform including the ability to mine and trade Ethereum, test smart contracts, and upload distributed applications (Dapps). With Frontier, canary contracts were used, and problematic contracts are given a value of 0 or 1. This functionality went against the decentralization narrative associated with blockchain development, however it allowed the developers to stop a transaction if it was problematic. The Frontier update was well-received by the developer community who started to use the platform for writing smart contracts and Dapps.

Homestead

Homestead is the second major version and the first hard fork of Ethereum. Released in early 2016, it included several changes: The canary contracts were removed, and the Mist wallet enabled users to hold and exchange ETH. This upgrade was implemented on block 1,150,000.

On the Ethereum Blog, Jeffery Wickle posted about the release: "We felt it was extremely important to clearly communicate to our users how we felt about the security of the network. Today, we're incredibly proud to announce that we are finally ready to remove the scratched-out word "safe" from our website as move into a new phase: Homestead."

There are several other important events that took place in the Ethereum timeline before the upgrade to Metropolis. So, I have included the upgrade where it appears in the chronological order.

DOA Attack
DAO was an investor-directed fund, launched in Apr 2016, and now an infamous application of the Ethereum blockchain. A project of blockchain and IoT company Slock, DAO used the DAO Framework 1.0 and allowed people to join as a voting member by investing ETH tokens.

"The developers of the DAO believed they could eliminate human error or manipulation of investor funds by placing decision-making power into the hands of an automated system and a crowdsourced process. Fueled by ether, the DAO was designed to allow investors to send money from anywhere in the world anonymously. The DAO would then provide those owners tokens, allowing them voting rights on possible projects." (Investopedia)

In May 2016, led by DAO, Ethereum was able to raise $150 million in a crowd sale, making it the largest crowdfunding effort ever. However, the success of the project also attracted unwanted attention. In June 2016, an anonymous hacker was able to access $50 million worth of ETH (3.6 million tokens) or 15% of all the Ether.

It was found that the attacker took advantage of a bug known as the "recursive call bug." The hacking happened on Jun 17. To understand the recursive function, let's consider a normal transaction. Normally, users could exchange DAO tokens with an equivalent amount in Ether. With the recursive function, the code repeated itself before the transaction was registered, enabling the exchange of a DAO token for more Ether than its equivalent value.

But the recursive call problem wasn't unknown to the developers. After the crowdfund campaign, there was the question of first dealing with the vulnerabilities of the platform or start to fund the 50+ proposals waiting for the project's token holders to vote on them. Addressing the bug issue, DAO co-creator Stephan Tual said that the DAO funds were not at risk due to the vulnerability.

It's important to mention that the Ethereum network wasn't faulty in this case. Besides the hacking, the DAO also had issues regarding its legal status. Like many of the projects based on the Ethereum blockchain that followed DAO, there was the question whether it should be regulated as a security. The hacking incident also contributed to many digital currencies exchanges de-listing the DAO token.

The DAO attacker was successful, but they would have to wait before receiving the stolen Ether. The smart contract exploited by the attacker had a function known as split schedule, the presence of which meant that the attacker would have to wait 28 days before they could withdraw their loot.

Formation of Ethereum Classic
This exploiting of the DEO smart contract divided the Ethereum community. Some were of the opinion that code is law, so it should not be changed under any circumstances. Others believed that the Ethereum protocol should be modified to create a new version of Ethereum and DAO should get back the stolen money through this "hard fork."

Those who were against the splitting argued that keeping the blockchain immutable makes it credible. Also, the Ethereum blockchain wasn't at fault in the incident, as the flaw was in the DAO coding. In other words, they wanted to protect the brand they had helped create.

On 17th June, Vitalik Buterin addressed the DAO attack proposing a software fork. He further said: "Miners and mining pools should resume allowing transactions as normal, wait for the soft fork code and stand ready to download and run it if they agree with this path forward for the Ethereum ecosystem. DAO token holders and Ethereum users should sit tight and remain calm. Exchanges should feel safe in resuming trading ETH."

In a soft fork, the newer version of the blockchain is compatible with the older version. In other words, it allows the new version of the blockchain to validate old blocks. However, the plan could not materialize because it was found that a soft fork would create 'Denial of Service' (DoS) attack vectors.

In response to the decision of a soft fork, the attacker or someone else released an open letter in which it was claimed that the Ether taken was legal and legal action would be taken if someone will try to invalidate the reward. This was followed by a statement saying that they will have a "smart contract to reward miners who oppose the soft fork and mines the transaction" if there was an attempt to steal his property.

On Jul 15, 2016, the Ethereum Foundation decided to hard fork Ethereum to return funds to their original accounts (wallets). In a hard fork, the new version of the blockchain does not interact with the old version. The hard fork was completed on Jul 20. The block number for the hard fork event was 19 20,000. The new version of the blockchain is Ethereum, and the original version of the platform is Ethereum Classic, and it preserves the DAO hack.

It's important to mention here that many community members were unhappy with fork. The Ethereum community mentioned their grievances with leadership of the Ethereum Foundation in the Ethereum Classic white paper. These grievances included, but were not limited to, rushing the "hard fork," which was consisted of a change in the blockchain's code that violated the properties of immutability, fungibility, the sanctity of the ledger, and deciding to exclude replay protection, an action which has unnecessarily cost exchanges and many users the ownership of their Ether tokens.

On the topic of immutability and fungibility, the paper says that immutability means "that only valid transactions agreed upon via a cryptographic protocol determined by mathematics are accepted by the network."

Tangerine Whistle
In Oct and Nov 2016, Ethereum implemented the Tangerine Whistle Spurious Dragon hard forks respectively. This purpose of the former was to increase the gas price of certain complex operations. The idea was to increase security by making DoS attacks more expensive for attackers. The fork was made on block 2,463,000. The latter fork was on block 2,675,000. It was done to address "important but less pressing matters such as further tuning opcode pricing to prevent future attacks on the network, enabling "debloat" of the Blockchain state, and adding replay attack protection" according to Coin telegraph.

Enterprise Ethereum Alliance
In Feb 2017, a group researchers and small and large companies, including JP Morgan and MS Microsoft, came together to form the Enterprise Ethereum Alliance. According to their official website, the alliance currently has over 250 member companies, over 1400 individual members, and its goal is to create "open, blockchain specifications that drive harmonization and interoperability for businesses and consumers worldwide."

The alliance has recently announced a token-based reward for members to encourage collaboration on projects. "Under the new system, businesses can earn, share, and redeem token-based rewards using Hyperledger Besu. Businesses can also dish out three types of tokens: "reputation", "reward", and "penalty," according to a Decrypt article.

Metropolis
The third stage of Ethereum development, Metropolis is further divided into Byzantium, Constantinople and Istanbul.

Byzantium

Byzantium was implemented in Oct 2017. The related block was 4,370,000 and it included nine Ethereum improvement Proposals (EIPs). The upgrade included the important feature zkSNARKS or "Zero-Knowledge Succinct Non-Interactive Argument of Knowledge" and a delay of "time bomb", a mechanism that is activated when needed to increase the difficulty level of block mining until no new blocks can be mined. Block geeks has provided a detailed explanation of zkSNARKS. The purpose of the time bomb mechanism was to facilitate the transition from a Proof of Work (PoW) system to a Proof of Stake (PoS) network.

Constantinople and St. Petersburg

The second stage Constantinople was planned for Oct 2017, but the developers decided to delay to early 2019. The update was scheduled at block number 7,280,000. According to a Ethereum blog post, the update has two names because "the original Constantinople network upgrade was postponed and two protocol upgrades will need to occur on the same block number in order to fix issues on various Ethereum test networks, such as Ropsten."

The Constantinople update has four EIPs, according to the post, including Bitwise shifting instructions in the Ethereum Virtual Machine (EVM) (discussed in the next chapter), enabling native functionality with protocol to make it "cheaper & easier to do certain things on chain" and Constantinople Difficulty Bomb Delay and Block Reward Adjustment to ensure the blockchain doesn't freeze before PoS is available.

The Constantinople EIPs were applied to test networks and the St. Petersburg update was done to remove EIPs from test networks. The update removed "net gas metering for SSTORE without dirty maps."

Istanbul

The Istanbul update was released on Sept 30, 2019. This latest fork of the Ethereum blockchain has 6 EIPs according to eth.wiki and the upgrades will: align the EVM opcodes costs with related computational costs, allow Ethereum and Zcash to interoperate, enable contracts to introduce creative functions. Zcash is a cryptocurrency using the zk-SNARKS hashing algorithm

Ethereum – The "World Computer"
Ethereum is presented as the world's computer. According to co-founder Dr. Gavin Wood, the computer has a number of features that make it a global computer: fundamentally the computer is not localized, unlike other physical and virtual machines. Unlike many computers, it's a multi-user computer, as people can log into it at the same time. It's accessible because it uses a relatively simple computer language; there is no question of transaction failing midway because the system is set in a way that a transaction either transmits or not, and we have the ability to check the address of the sender.

Of course, moving forward, the Ethereum community will play a big role and making it possible for Ethereum to achieve its goal of becoming the world computer. Critics of the project say that the goals set by Ethereum are not clearly defined. However, the project has a rather large community of developers behind it who continue to innovate.

How Ethereum Works

The Transaction Diagram

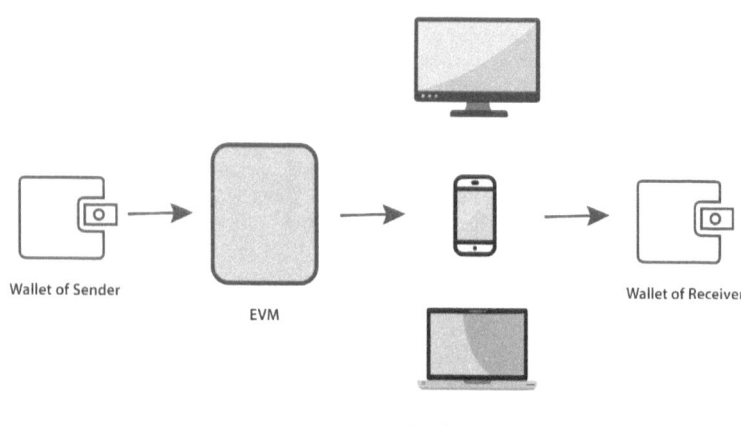

To understand how transactions, take place on the Ethereum blockchain, let's consider the simple example given in the diagram above. this example involves the sender sending the Ethereum networks native cryptocurrency ether to someone.

Step 1: In the first step, the sender uses the public key of the receiver to send Ether.

Step 2: The request is received by the Ethereum Virtual Machine (EVM), which is a quasi-Turing complete machine*. The hash value of the transaction is found and the transaction is transmitted to the distributed network of nodes

Step 3: The nodes validate and store the transaction.

Step 4: In the final step, the sender uses their private key to access the Ether they have received.

*Named after Alan Turning, turning complete is an abstract idea of a machine that can perform any calculation. EVM is not a complete Turning machine because it's computing power is restricted by gas or fuel. However, EVM uses opcodes, which enables it to be officially called Turing complete. In other words, it can make 'almost' any calculation provided there's enough capacity to do so.

Nodes
Instead of a centralized server that stores all the account information, a decentralized network like Ethereum has thousands of different nodes that act collectively act as the server. To understand the data synchronization by Ethereum nodes let's consider how data is stored on the Ethereum blockchain.

The data structure used to store is known as a Merkle tree. This structure consists of the root node, a set of intermediate nodes, and a bunch of leaf nodes containing the underlying data. A key is assigned to each value stored in the tree. The key can be used to track the path from the root to the underlying value.

Full and Lightweight Nodes
The full node downloads and stores the complete transaction history of the blockchain, verifies all blocks and account states, and stores the recent state for initial synchronization.

In contrast, a light node only stores the header of a block. The nodes can verify data against the state roots in the header.

The nodes cannot make changes to the data because of the way the protocol is written. With a centralized system, you may pay a fee to the system owner for their services and expenses. With Ethereum, the nodes receive compensation for validating data.

Distribution of Ethereum Nodes
You can run an Ethereum node and validating transactions by using an Ethereum client. Given on ethernodes.org, the total number of nodes at the time of acquiring the information were 6627. The two most popular clients for running nodes are Geth and Parity-Ethereum. Out of the 6627, 4510 (67.93%) are with Geth and 2070 (31.18%) are with parity-Ethereum. The hardware required, storage and synchronization time will depend on the type of node you choose.

In terms of the operating systems used for running the nodes, Linux is the most popular by far with 91.66% or 6076 nodes running on the network. Windows and Mac OS are in 2nd and 3rd place with 401 and 77 nodes respectively.

In terms of the type of network used for the nodes, Hosting is the most popular with 4654 or 70.18% of the nodes followed by the Residential with 1582 (23.86% and business with 213 (3.21%) of the nodes. There are also 73 nodes on cellular and 44 on college networks.

Out of the 4654 networks on Hosting, Amazon.com is used by 1645 or 35.3%. The other major competitor is Alibaba better 731 (15.71%). In the residential category, Chinese companies dominate the market, with China Telecom with 284 (17.93%) and China Unicom Liaoning with 70 (4.42%) in the top positions. Out of the Business clients, Google34 (16.04%), LG DACOM Corporation12 (5.66%) and Verizon Fios Business7 (3.30% are no.1, 2 and 3 respectively.

Majority of the Ethereum nodes are located in the United States (above 26%). China is in 2nd place with over 16% of the nodes. Germany Singapore and Hong Kong are fairly close to each other with about 9 percent, 8% and 6.5 % of the nodes.

In terms of the versions of the popular clients used, Geth stats look like as follows: 1.8.23822 (18.23%), 1.9.6759 (16.83%), 1.8.27757 (16.78%). Parity-Ethereum's popular versions include 2.5.9383 (18.50%), 2.2.11163 (7.87%), and 2.6.4160 (7.73%). Geth and parity-Ethereum are by far the most the ghost clients, but there are other options available as well. These include, but are not limited to, parity 16 (0.24%), Getc 10 (0.15%), and Besu 7 (0.11%).

Of course, all of these starts are ever changing because of new clients becoming a part of the network and some clients leaving the network as well.

Consensus Protocol

Like Bitcoin, Ethereum also uses the proof of work consensus protocol. As mentioned in the first book, the proof of work mechanism was developed before the development of Bitcoin, but it was popularized by its use as Bitcoin's consensus protocol. In a proof of work system, the miners solve a cryptographic puzzle to validate the transaction. In exchange of their work, they get a reward in the blockchain's native currency, Ether in the case of Ethereum.

The Mining Process

In a stepwise manner, the process happens as follows: minors find a hash value that matches the transaction transmitted to the Ethereum network. Then, a miner beats other miners to the solution of the hash to receive the reward. Finally, the transaction becomes a part of a block.

Nonce Value

The nonce number is the number that miners are solving for when we talk about Ethereum or other blockchains.

"A nonce is an abbreviation for "number only used once," which is a number added to a hashed—or encrypted—block in a blockchain that, when rehashed, meets the difficulty level restrictions." (Investopedia)

To understand this number, let's understand the mining process in specific terms. The mining process involves running the the unique header of the block through a hash function. The hash function provides the miner with a random string of numbers and letters with the nonce value changed. If the miner is able to guess the correct hash, they will receive the reward. The next step in the process will be the broadcasting of the block to the nodes and the network for validation and inclusion in the ledger off the blockchain. The losing miners will stop work on the block and move on to the next one.

Comparison b/w PoW and PoS

In a PoW system, the mining capacity depends on the computational power you have at your disposal. In a PoS system, miners are replaced by validators, and the validating capacity that relates to how much stake you have in the network. Like miners receive rewards in a PoW system, validators collect transaction fees. Another notable comparison is the amount of energy needed. In terms of the security you get with the consensus protocols , PoS systems are more secure because they are less susceptible to attacks like the 51% attack, an attack where attackers can manipulate the block chain by gaining control of over 51% of the activity taking place on the blockchain.

Mining Reward

Miners used to receive 5 ethers (ETH) for verifying transactions. However, with Ethereum's rapid increase in price starting from 2016, the reward was reduced to 2 ETH. This practice is not uncommon in the cryptocurrency world. For instance, Bitcoin halves their block reward once every four years. The idea behind this policy is to protect the interest of ETH holders. By reducing the reward, you reduce new coins being issued, in theory. Less supply translates to less sell pressure, allowing those holding ETH to anticipate an increase in value.

Mining Difficulty

The difficulty to mine is an adjustable feature in the Ethereum blockchain. The algorithm can adjust the difficulty of the problem so that the time required to mine Ether remains in the same range. For Ethereum, the current mining level is around four blocks per minute. It's also noteworthy that mining Ethereum is faster compared to mining Bitcoin. This has a lot to do with the types of blocks permitted in the blockchain. Besides the parent and child blocks, Ethereum also allows the inclusion of "uncle blocks."

Ethash

Ethereum's PoW is called 'ethash' and it's developed by modifying the Dagger-Hashimoto algorithm. Ethash is based on a randomly generated dataset known as a DAG (Directed Acyclic Graph). DAG "is used in all Ethash coins, like Ethereum, Ethereum Classic, Ubiq and other coins to provide proof of the work done. DAG file is generated every mining epoch and it increases from epoch to epoch," according to Investoon. One epoch equals 30,000 blocks.

ASIC Mining

ASIC mining is a term that became popular with Bitcoin mining. The Bitcoin algorithm requires a simple SHA-256 computation. This resulted in special ASIC chips that could process enormous quantities of hashes, which in turn made ordinary miners using standard hardware redundant. In other words, the use of these large mining operations centralized mining. This is the case with Bitcoin; however, Ethereum is also facing a similar challenge with Bitmain introducing ASIC rigs for Ethereum. However, Ethereum is in a better position to combat the threat from these mining rigs. The reason for this is the use of DAGs. The memory and CPU requirements are lower. Also, somewhere in 2019 to 2021, Ethereum plans to move away from PoW to the Proof of Stake (PoS) mechanism.

Expansion in Capacity

According to a Decrypt article, in response to an increase in traffic, mainly due to controversial stablecoin Tether and the Fair Win gambling game, the mining community has increased Ethereum's network capacity to enable a higher number of transactions per second – 25% more. It was recently revealed that 25% of all Ethereum activity are Tether transactions, adds the article.

Ethereum Wallets

If you're looking to trade Ethereum you will start with placing your Ethereum in the wallet. The wallet will have a public key, which will be a collection of numbers and letters that you give people to send you money. Along with the public key, you will have a private key. This is the key that will unlock the money you have received. There are different kinds of wallets for crypto currencies. Also, you can create your own wallet using the Ethereum platform .

The two main types of wallets are hot and cold wallets. A hot wallet stores your keys online, making it possible for you to access them wherever you are. The other option is that of code wallets. These wallets are offline, unless you take them online. If you want to try and create your own wallet, you can do so with Ethereum's own wallet creation tool My Ether Wallet, which is a web-based wallet. Besides web-based wallets like MyEtherWallet and Lumi Wallet Web, you can choose from desktop wallets, such as MetaMask and Exodus, Mobile wallets, such as Coinomi and Lumi Wallet, and paper wallets, a wallet which is simply codes written on a piece of paper.

Ether

Ether (ETH) is the native currency of Ethereum. Ethereum.org defines ETH as "digital money" that you can send "instantly and cheaply." However, ether is designed to be a little different than your typical cryptocurrency. To understand ether let's compare it through to the market leader Bitcoin.

Fuel for the Network

Like bitcoin, ether is traded publicly, mineable, and doesn't require a third party for transactions. But, unlike bitcoin, ether provides "fuel" or "gas" for the Dapps present on the Ethereum network.

In other words, Ether is the transaction fee you pay the network for processing transactions. Let's say you have a decentralized app running on the Ethereum network. If you want to make a change to that app, you will create a request for that change which will then be processed by the network. The ether will be the charges for engaging the computational resources of the network.

What is the purpose of collecting this fee? This fee is used to incentivize the nodes present in the network. As discussed above nodes validate transactions and receive a reward in return. Besides the validators, ether is also a form of payment for the developers developing apps on the block chain.

Ether Calculation

Who decides how much fuel is required for a given task? The amount in Ether someone pays is equal to the computational power and time that transaction will require.

This gas price is the cost of one unit of gas, given as Gwei (1 ETH = 1,000,000,000 Gwei). Ether does not have a cap, like some other crypto currencies. Initially, it was capped at 18,000,000 Ether per year.

How to Buy Ether

If you're not an ETH miner, then you will need to use an exchange to acquire it or use a platform that rewards you in Ether for perfuming tasks. Some of the exchanges selling ETH are Binance, Coinbase, Cex.io, Gemini, and Kraken. ETH exchanges can be divided into three main types:

Trading platforms: These online platforms are convenient, and the fees are also usually lower.

Brokers: Brokers sell directly and are more expensive than trading platforms.</p>

Marketplaces: P2P platforms allow you to negotiate with the seller. The service charges are higher.

Exchanges

Coinbase

Coinbase is an exchange company (GDAX), and wallet that allows you to exchange Bitcoin, Ethereum, Litecoin, and other digital assets with fiat currencies. The popular choice for many, the platform has over 30 million users. There are also developing their Coinbase prime platform for institutional clients. For individuals, they have the Coinbase Pro platform.

CEX.io is also a well-established exchange that deals in Ethereum and also offers a trading platform. The exchange rate difference can be up to 7% between using the brokerage and trading platform. The platform provides you with several payment options, including Visa, MasterCard, ACH, SWIFT, and SEPA transfers and cryptocurrency.

Bitstamp

Bitstamp is an established European trading platform and brokerage that offers Ethereum. The trading fees will vary depending on the amount you trade, ranging from zero point 0.1% two 0.25%. Bitstamp recently announced that it will be using BitGo's storage services for storing the its assets. "With BitGo Custody, Bitstamp's assets will be secured on 100% cold storage technology in bank-grade class III vaults and protected by BitGo's $100 million (USD) insurance policy," according to a release.

Binance

Binance is a crypto to crypto exchange for trading over 100 cryptocurrencies, and also a brokerage service. The crypto trading platform Also has its own crypto currency called Binance Coin (BNB) Which was launched on the Ethereum blockchain but was later migrated to the exchanges on blockchain called the Binance Chain. You can use BNB to pay trade fees.

Smart Contracts

In some ways, smart contracts are like regular contracts, but there are some major difference as well. Like any regular contract, the smart contract can indicate a transaction or agreement between parties. But, unlike regular contacts, smart contracts do not require you to disclose who you are by real or pseudo name, and, in case of Ethereum, the contract is validated by multiple nodes or validators. It's also important to note here that Smart contracts are immutable, meaning that they are created for ever and their record is also available for verification forever. Regarding the middleman in your transaction, there is no traditional middleman who you will pay to validate the transaction, but there is a transaction fee, which according to Ethereum, goes towards that developers and validators.

Example

Let's consider the example off online marketplace similar to eBay. For every item you sell on this platform, you have to pay one or multiple fees for doing business through that platform and follow the rules set by the platform. In case of smart contracts, you don't have any third-party managing buyer and seller requests and setting rules for the contract between the two parties like the traditional online marketplace.

Smart Contract History

The phrase and concept of "smart contracts" was developed by Nick Szabo, a legal scholar and cryptographer who researched digital contracts and digital currency.

Szabo designed bit gold, a mechanism for a decentralized digital currency in 1998 but never implemented the concept. Bit gold also introduced the concept of using computing power to solve cryptographic puzzles, with solutions becoming a part of a public registry.

"Anything that works well as a proof-of-work function, producing a specific binary string such that it can be proved that generating that string was computationally costly, will work," states Szabo, according to IEEE Spectrum article.

The challenges or puzzles were chained together because the solved puzzle would become a part of the next challenge. The consensus mechanism for bit gold involved majority of the involved parties accepting the solution before the system processed the next puzzle.

Szabo was against a central authority controlling the network transactions. "I was trying to mimic as closely as possible in cyberspace the security and trust characteristics of gold, and chief among those is that it doesn't depend on a trusted central authority," he added.

The need for a central authority with digital coins arose from the design problem of "double-spending," mentions the article. "Double-spending is the risk that a digital currency can be spent twice. It is a potential problem unique to digital currencies because digital information can be reproduced relatively easily by savvy individuals who understand the blockchain network and the computing power necessary to manipulate it" (Investopedia). To solve this issue, most e-cash setups gave up a part of their control to a central authority that would track balances of accounts.

Like Ethereum, Bitcoin also has smart contracts, but they were only useful for transferring currency transfer. So how do smart contracts work on the Ethereum blockchain?

How Smart Contracts Work

Ethereum's coding language enables developers to write their own smart contracts, as explained in an example below. Solidity

To understand how smart contracts work, let's consider how general accounts work on the block chain. Like the example of Bitcoin given in the 1st eBook, you have nodes validating the transactions between accounts according to a consensus mechanism. So, if you are looking to send Ether too someone , your transaction goes through the same process as a Bitcoin transaction in the sense that it will be validated by all nodes on the network.

So how are smart contracts different from a regular process on the Ethereum blockchain? smart contracts are different because while they are also validated by the nodes present on the network to confirm that they follow the protocols , you can program these contracts according to your requirements and use these contracts in a multitude of ways besides currency transactions, including managing agreements, storing information, etc. Unlike the private key system for accessing accounts that you have with regular transactions, you can set your own criteria including not requiring a private key to access an account.

The presence of smart contracts on a decentralized network provides you with a lot of flexibility and the presence of a blockchain network that facilitates smart contracts makes it possible to fast track a project. We have so far discussed smart contracts as a single contract. In a real a project, you may need to combine several smart contracts.

Smart contracts also help you get element of bias and human error out of the process. For example, if you have a program to reward your employees, there's a chance you may reward someone not based on the criteria you have set but based on how good your relationship is with them. With a smart contract you can enter your criteria and take care of the rewards without any biases. Also, in this case, your employees will also know that there is a transparent process for distribution of rewards.

Language for Smart Contracts
The Ethereum smart contracts are written in solidarity, an object-oriented high-level programming language "influenced by C++, Python and JavaScript and is designed to target the Ethereum Virtual Machine (EVM). Solidity is statically typed, supports inheritance, libraries and complex user-defined types among other features," according to the following Solidity resource.

Anatomy of a Smart Contract
Here is a basic example of a smart contract that allows you to store a number, as given on the following Solidity resource.

pragma solidity >=0.4.0 <0.7.0;

contract SimpleStorage {uint storedData;function set(uint x) public {storedData = x;}

function get() public view returns (uint) {return storedData;}

The first line mentions that the source code is for Solidity version 0.4.0, or a more recent version of the language up to, but not including version 0.7.0.

The next line declares a state variable called "storedData" and data type: "uint" (unsigned integer of 256 bits). The functions "set" and "get" allow modification or retrieval of the value of the variable. This contract allows you to store a number that anyone can access from anywhere.

https://ethereum.stackexchange.com/questions/71954/can-anyone-explain-how-smart-contract-gets-validated

Are Smart Contracts Smart?
Technically speaking smart contracts do not have any functionality that makes them smarter than any other type of contract. Like a regular contract, their design depends on the abilities of the person writing the contract. Somewhat also argue that the word contract isn't suitable either, because these contracts lack the subjectivity that is a part of many contracts.

Are Smart Contracts Smart Legal Contracts?
In terms of the legal status of smart contracts, legality in there depending on whether or not the smart contract fulfilled the applicable legal requirements. In other words, just because something is declared a smart contract, it does not qualify as a legal contract between involved parties.

According to a Hackernoon article, Dave Michels, researcher with the Cloud Legal Project says, "If the counterparty is an ordinary consumer, a judge may find that simply referring to machine-readable code does not provide sufficient notice of contractual terms to be binding." In contrast, "if the counterparty is a Solidity expert, a judge might find that the human-readable terms of the agreement legitimately deferred to the machine-readable code."

Applications of Ethereum

20 Ethereum Use Cases

Ethereum is one of the most used platforms for blockchain and cryptocurrency related projects. these projects span all categories, from internet essentials and social media networks to business and finance. in the following lines I have included some of the most promising Ethereum use cases from different categories.

1. Status

Status is a messaging app that uses public and private keys and allows you to do public, private and group chats and it also features a Ethereum wallet. For private messages, it has the Messenger called whisper, a peer-to-peer dark routing enabled tool you can use for "easy and efficient multi-casting and broadcasting; low-level partially-asynchronous communications; and low-value traffic reduction or retardation," according to Status.

Here p2p communication means that your messages aren't processed by or stored on a server. Dark means that no one can track your messages in certain modes. Multicast means that, you can broadcast a message to the whole network by using only one receiver's public key.

To create an account, you don't need to provide any phone number or email. You use the Network with only your keys . regarding the storage of the keys status says " the first BIP44 key is saved in a keystore json file locally on your device. This file is encrypted with the password you choose for your Status account and only accessible by the Status app." Status also as has a feature for cold storage. You can learn more about the key card cold storage here. It's also important to note that Because of how accounts work on status, you cannot recover your password if you forget it.

2. MetaMask

An Ethereum wallet in your browser, MetaMask connects you to your favorite Dapps directly from your browser. MetaMask runs a light node on the browser, and it's is an easy-to-use tool, because all features are clearly laid out. The extension is available for Chrome, Firefox, Opera and the new Brave browser.

MetaMask is compatible with local client wallets and hardware wallets, and it's directly connected to two exchanges: Coinbase, where you can buy Ether, and ShapeShift, where you can buy Ether or ERC20 tokens. MetaMask comes with an identity vault that helps you manage your accounts on different sites and sign transactions. Account back up is also available: They give you a list of words called seed phrases. You can use these phrases to reset lost account information. Being an online wallet, one of the main risks with MetaMask is security.

3. Opera

Opera is a browser with a built-in crypto wallet. You download the browser for Android and more recently for iOS. the browser will automatically show you tokens that are ERC20 compliant. Regarding the wallet keys Opera says that the keys are stored in your device and there do not backup or transmit the keys. Opera has started with Ethereum and plants to include other crypto currencies and data platforms in the future. In case you lose the Phone on which you had downloaded opera , you will use the backup phrase you receive after setting up the wallet to recover your wallet. Besides ETH and ERC-20 tokens, ERC-721 collectibles and unique tokens.

4. Golem

Golem is an open source, decentralized network that connects people with surplus computational power 2 people who are looking for it .   For example, if you have a large task, you can split it into small tasks, and use someone else's computer to complete this section as you complete the rest, thus completing the whole task faster than the normal duration. The people sharing their computers with others will receive the compensation then their computer is used. golem and receives transaction fee for each transaction.

5. Local Ethereum

Local Ethereum is a peer to peer network or exchanging ETH. according to the official website, majority of trades complete in a few minutes Dependent and depend on the payment method. in terms of payment methods, you have a variety of options. also, the network is available in over 130 countries .

The format of the local aetherian allows anyone to bid on your ETH. During the transaction Ethereum is placed in their escrow, which is a decentralized Ethereum smart contract. You receive the payment outside yes, the platform. And confirm on the platform to release their scroll . All the conversation you have with the other party on the platform is private and protected by is self-destructing secret key. local Ethereum is compatible with meta mask , Status and several other wallets. Local Ethereum also have their own web wallet .

Regarding the fees, the website says that the charges are "0.25% fee for the maker (the person who placed the offer listing) and 0.75% for the taker (the person responding to the offer). The reason for the significant discount on makers is because we want to encourage people to place offers."

6. Compound

Compound is an open source protocol for money markets on the Ethereum network. It works as a "liquidity pool," because instead of lending to someone you supply liquidity to a market and others borrow from that market. According to the Compound white paper, Money markets hard pools of assets with interest rates that are development with algorithm and based on demand and supply of the asset . As the person supplying or borrowing their cert, you deceive received a floating interest rate .

The money market is unique to then it hit him Ethereum asset , such as an ERC-20 token. For borrowing, assets the protocol uses collateral to set how much you can borrow. You can use each of your balances in the protocol (ERC-20 tokens called cTokens) to borrow assets.

Some of the interfaces that have integrated the compound protocol include Zerion, Coinbase Wallet, InstaDapp and DeFi Saver.

7. Bounties Network
According to the Bounties Network website " We make it easy to outsource any task, completed by top talent from anywhere in the world. Some examples of tasks organizations and individuals have had success with are: code, content creation, music, art, social impact, research and more. Rewards can be paid in any ERC20 token on the Ethereum blockchain."

How to create a bounty: For a bounty you provide: a description, expected deliverables, full requirements, tokens for the reward and for loading the bounty, the bounty category, and level of difficulty of the bounty. After a bounty is created, it become a part of the pool of open bounties on the network.

If you like to complete a bounty, you can apply to start working on the bounty, if required. When the work is complete, you will submit the files so the task creator can review it.

8. Ethlance
The Ethlance platform is a marketplace for freelancers and companies in the digital sector. According to their website, you'll have to install the MetaMask browser extension. On the platform, you can search the job offers created on the platform and post a job request. Job posters select from the applicants. When you complete an order, payment will be made as Ether. This process is similar to standard freelancing platforms. however, the difference is that there are no membership fees or transaction fees . as a platform based on Ethereum , there is gas fee, but this fee is lower compared to or to pay on standard platforms .

9. Minds
Minds is a social network where you can earn rewards for your contributions. The Minds token is an ERC-20 for rewards, p2p content subscriptions and advertising. The token distribution process allows it to scale autonomously. "We reward you for the energy you put in, whether that is creating great content, being active or helping develop our code," mentions the website. If you want to use the network for promotions, you can do so by exchanging your tokens, with one token equalling 1k views. You can also target the whole network or a specific audience. Minds also allows you to build your own customized social network.

10. CryptoKitties
One of the first blockchain games, CryptoKitties enables users to "collect and breed oh-so-adorable creatures that we call CryptoKitties! Each kitty has a unique genome that defines its appearance and traits. Players can breed their kitties to create new furry friends and unlock rare cattributes," according to their website.

Besides playing the game, you can make money by selling your CryptoKitties. The amount of money you will make will depend on different factors. According to a The Next Web article, one cat, called Dragon, was sold for 600 ETH (about $170,000 approximately), breaking the record of Founder Cat #18, which went for 253 ETH ($110,000).

The game is compatible with Chrome and Firefox 4 Mac Linux on PC. The main way people buy cryptokitties in the game are through auctions. If you're looking to breed guards then you will need a sire and a dame. it transaction fees associated with each building session.

11. Dolomite DEX

A new project, Dolomite DEX is a decentralized exchange that enables you to trade directly from a noncustodial Ethereum wallets. The exchange also features an integrated portfolio manager, where you can enter your Ethereum address to check your balances and transfer. There is also the option to connect your bank account or debit card to buy cryptocurrencies and to exchange your cryptos back into USD. For margin traders, the platform offers margin trading of up to 5x.

12. IDEX

IDEX's " a decentralized exchange for trading Ethereum (ERC-20) tokens. IDEX combines the speed of centralization with the security of blockchain settlement," according to their website.

The smart contract of IDEX is designed to only allow the exchange to tranmsit signed trades to the blockchain. This means IDEX can separate trading from final settlement. The exchange updates balances in real-time, while enabling you to simultaneously use your private keys to authorize trades. IDEX cannot access your funds without cryptographically signed permission from you.

13. Uport

Uport, an ethereum-based identity protocol, provides tools for individuals and organizations to share data in a trusted and secure manner. There tools are for user-controlled data, scalable and secure data exchanges and integrated infrastructure for enterprises, consortiums, and Web3.

The Uport mobile app enables users to create a personal identity on the Ethereum blockchain network. The Uport identity provides a secure exchange of information with the additional security of Ethereum blockchain. The identity includes the facts about a person (or app, organization, device) which are needed when interacting with smart contracts and other Uport identities. This could be either off the chain or on the chain, making it a self-sovereign identity.

In the traditional public key cryptography system if the private key is lost, the identity is lost. The Uport registry is a persistent key, which is a single smart contract shared by all Uport identities. This is simple to operate and could be used for off-chain data sharing and verification of identity.

Uport has partnered with different companies and also with government. According to a Coindesk report, uPort's partnered is with the government of Zug for a pilot program to register citizens' IDs on Ethereum. They completed the first registry in Nov last year. In another project, uPort and Microsoft partnered helped Brazil's Ministry of Planning in verifying notarized documents. Uport has recently partnered with PWC and Onfido for a digital ID project.

14. Augur

Augur is as a P2P prediction market platform built on the Ethereum blockchain. Because of its decentralized nature, users have control over what is put up for betting, unlike other platforms where betting topics are selected by the site.

In the Augur market, you can sell and buy shares of the outcome of a future event. For example, you can be a Market Creator and create a question (topic) for the election taking place in the country and give the candidates as the options for others to bet on. As the topic creator, you will set the Augur price that traders will pay to buy and sell shares in this market, set a reporter and a resolution resource.

The Augur price for shares ranging from 0 to 1 ETH per share. A bid closer to 1 ETH limit means that the participant is confident about the outcome. for example if the place 0.6 ETH, it means that they are 60% sure that their chosen candidate will win the election. If you bet correctly, your winnings will be equal to the number of shares you have when the market closes.

The role of the reporter will be to share their opinion about which way the elections are going. They use Augur coin, or Reputation tokens (REP) to report. If they report correctly, They earn REP for their effort. Of course, you can also place your bet on one of the a topic listed in the market. You can place a bet with ETH or any other Ethereum currency.

Augur gave a preview of its upcoming platform overhaul at Devcon 5. The changes are expected in Q1 of 2020. Revealing the news on stage at Devcon 5 in Osaka, Japan, Augur founder Joey Krug said that, "While Augur may be slow, expensive, and clunky today—that won't be the case much longer."

15. Ujo
Ujo is an Ethereum-based platform for musicians. "Our open platform uses blockchain technology to create a transparent and decentralized database of rights and rights owners, automating royalty payments using smart contracts and cryptocurrency," according to Ujo.

As an artist, you can register an account for free and specify all the important details, including the royalties, inspiration, content creation, and licensing. You have complete control of the licensing terms, including the price of the streams, downloads, and syncs. And, you can also decide whether you want instantaneous or periodical payments. Also, if you don't like to charge for your music, you can create a "license" for free use of your music. There is however no option to delete your music from the platform, so make sure you upload content that you want to have there.

You can also extend your license to incorporate a wide range of additional functions, such as programmatic contracts, variable pricing, and payment routing. You receive 100% of the amount you sell, but it costs a small fee to list your music on the network. According to Ujo, this fee is associated with the gas required by the Ethereum protocol.

"It was one of the first times blockchain was used for anything else besides trading crypto, and that was pretty exciting," says Alexander Attar, the project lead at Ujo, according to Decrypt. "We saw that music could provide a catalyst for blockchain technology."

16. Marble.
Marble is an open-source bank that lends Ether and tokens to low-risk protocols. An article by cofounder Max Wolff explains its details: Their Flash lending integration on the Ethereum Mainnet lets you borrow Ether and ERC20 tokens for arbitrage on Ethereum. You can, for instance, use flash lending to make arbitrage trades on a decentralized exchange DEX, such as 0x or Kyber.

"With flash lending, a trader can borrow from the Marble bank, buy a token on one DEX, sell the token on another DEX for a higher price, repay the bank, and pocket the arbitrage profit all in a single atomic transaction," adds the article.

The developer have also launched Polaris, an on-chain price oracle powered by Uniswap, a decentralized exchange and automated market maker. The tool is designed to be accurate, resistant to price manipulation, and self-sustaining," according to co founder Mykel Pereira.

17. MakerDAO
Maker DAO consists of a decentralized stable coin, collateral loans and community governance. It's a smart contract platform that backs and stabilizes the value of their cryptocurrency Dai, a stable coin, "through a dynamic system of Collateralized Debt Positions (CDPs), autonomous feedback mechanisms, and appropriately incentivized external actors," mentions their white paper. Being a stable coin, the cryptocurrency is pegged to an asset, a 1:1 peg with the USD, in Dai's case.

"We believe that stable digital assets like Dai are essential to realizing the full potential of blockchain technology. Unlike other Stablecoins, Dai is completely decentralized," adds the paper. You can buy Dai from brokers or exchanges, and make a steady, low-risk return on your holdings through the "Dai Savings Rate."

Maker DAO is considered one of the most successful operations built on Ethereum, as it holds nearly 2 % of all Ether within its smart contracts. Dai's worth $77 million have been issued over its system. The operational mechanism ensures that enough capital is always retained against the amount of funds taken out. When the interest rate is low, more people borrow. Similarly, if interest rate is high, it would be less attractive to people for borrowing. MakerDAO will be launching a new version of its programmatic stablecoin DAI soon: The MakerDAO Foundation CEO Rune Christensen announced a Nov 18 launch date at the Devcon Ethereum developer conference in Osaka, Japan.

18. Gitcoin
Gitcoin "connects freelance developers with online jobs solving bug bounties, building features and designing creatives paid in crypto," according to their website.

At present, most open-source software development start as passion project and only a small number of developers are there to maintain the project. Gitcoin aims to develop a community where developers come to offer their services and get compensated for it. The contributors are called Bounty and the Funders are called Repo maintainers on Gitcoin.

"Gitcoin and ConsenSys Labs will host a three-week virtual hackathon called Beyond Blockchain from June 24–July 10. The event gives participants the chance to win prizes in Ethereum and ERC-20 tokens posted as bounties on Gitcoin. According to the announcement, the event focuses on bringing blockchain tools and technologies to a wider audience, " reported Cryptoslate.

19. Etheremon
Etheremon is a game Similar to the Pokémon franchise, but in a decentralized space. " It creates a world of Mons (Etheremons) where you can capture, train, transform, and trade them with others," according to their website.

The monsters, called a Mon, can be trained. Majority of Mons are limited in supply, which creates opportunities for trading Mons. Also, Mons in advanced forms need to be evolved, making them hard to come by.

Secondly, you can mine EMONT, the in-game cryptocurrency. These ERC-20 token can be traded for Ether and then used for purchasing Mons and other items. The company hopes to increase demand for EMOT in the future by making it the only in-game currency.

According to a Yourstory post, talking about the game co-founder Nedrick Ngo said, "It's like an adventure. Most people go around in the game collecting monster stuff. A few months later, after our presales of the digital assets of the monster, we started moving a lot of features around the core, which is a monster. Most of our players are now playing on a desktop to use some application call, which will help start your wallet and help you to make a transaction with a smart contract. You can also do it with some mobile browsers. "

20. Super Player
Based on the blockchain game, Krypton Knight, SuperPlayer is a decentralized MMO game you can play by yourself or as a team. Besides exploring and battling, you can also start a business, providing different supplies to other players, and build your own empire.

The Future of Ethereum

Challenges and Limitations
Scalability

Scalability is a well-documented issue with Ethereum and it's also acknowledged by Vitalik Buterin. Scalability is also a challenge that Ethereum has in common with Bitcoin, so that's one less differentiating factor between the two platforms.

Invest in Blockchain reports a conversation in which Vitalik talks about the challenges: "As far as the big problems, my top three at this point are probably scalability, privacy and usability. So, scalability – the Ethereum blockchain right now can process 15 transactions per second." He also added that they will need to process 100,000 transactions per second.

The problem arises because Ethereum must make sure that all the transactions are accurately recorded. Of course, for this purpose they used validating nodes that stored the information. Data storage becomes a problem because the nodes must have the capacity to store the ever-increasing amount of data resulting from every transaction happening on the network, as required by the proof of work mechanism. As mentioned in the consensus protocol section, Ethereum does have light nodes and full nodes, but despite their presence the system is still not able to process transactions fast enough. Also, full nodes are still the most secure way of validating transactions but they also need more computing power than light nodes, making them less reachable to small, independent nodes.

The result of this limitation is that projects may have to make it harder for its users to use their products so they can send fewer transactions to the Ethereum network for validation. One example of this happening was the launch of the CryptoKitties project. The wildly popular launch of the project put additional pressure on the Ethereum network, which was not able to handle those transactions. As a result, CryptoKitties had to increase the price.

Of course, Ethereum is looking to completely move away from the proof of work system, but until that happens, the scalability problem with the current platform needs to be addressed. According to Vitalik, " There are two major kinds of strategies that we're working on for scalability. One is layer-one scaling and the other is layer-two scaling…And our solution to this, called sharding, basically means that you split up the different transactions to randomly selected, different groups of computers…And that can increase scalability by maybe a factor of 1,000 or so, but then potentially even more, much later down the road."

Sharding

As mentioned above, one of the solutions to the scalability problem is sharding. Sharding is a well-known technique in database management. With Ethereum, sharding will help to reduce the dependency on full nodes. However, sharding is not a flawless solution. In sharding, one node will store part of the information and will depend on another node if it needs additional information. This means that the node will have to trust another node, thus removing the trustless feature of the blockchain.

Hacking

Starting from the DAO attack mentioned before in the book, there have been numerous hackings of cryptocurrency projects. According to research by U.K. and Singapore researchers, titled "Finding The Greedy, Prodigal, and Suicidal Contracts at Scale," many smart Contracts are vulnerable to hacking.

After examining 970,898 smart contracts, they found that 34,200 of the contracts were easy targets for hacking. Moreover, they found that "In addition, 6,239 Ether (about $5.6 million) is locked inside posthumous contracts currently on the blockchain, of which 313 Ether have been sent to dead contracts after they have been killed," according to an Investopedia publication.

According to the paper, the three main categories of smart contracts are:

- Greedy: "31,201 greedy candidates (1,524 distinct), which amounts to around 3.2%of the contracts present on the blockchain."
- Prodigal Contracts: "1,504 candidates contracts (438 distinct) which may leak Ether to an arbitrary Ethereum address, with a true positive rate of around 97%."
- Suicidal Contracts: 1495 contracts, out of which 403 were distinct.

Proof of Stake

Proof of stake will help with scaling because there will no longer be a need to use large amounts of computational power. However, some believe that the protocol will lead to security challenges.

Off-Chain Transactions

In this system, majority of transactions will happen on off-chain micropayment channels, which will lift the burden from the Ethereum blockchain. As a result, there won't be a need to increase Ethereum computational capabilities by a lot. There are previous examples off chain platforms with cryptocurrencies, specifically the Lightning Network with Bitcoin .

Leader

Vitalik Buterin is the face of the operation and a capable person. However, over-reliance on one person can be problematic.

Ethereum 2.0

This is the serenity update off the blockchain protocol. According to the official website, Ethereum 2.0 will entail the following:

Phases

Ethereum's Upgrade comes along with Sharding, Proof-of-stake solutions (Beacon Chain, Casper the Friendly Finality Gadget {FFG}), eWASM (a new virtual machine), Plasma, Raiden and much more. The upgrade will be launched in phases:

Phase 0

This phase involves the launch of Beacon Chain. Beacon Chain will manage the Casper Proof-of-Stake protocol for itself and all of the shard chains.

This entails: "There are a number of aspects to this: managing validators and their stakes; nominating the chosen block proposer for each shard at each step; organizing validators into committees to vote on the proposed blocks; applying the consensus rules; applying rewards and penalties to validators; and, being an anchor point on which the shards register their states to facilitate cross-shard transactions," according to Ben Edgington.

One of the key features of Phase 0 is the introduction of ETH2. Currently, a validator cannot withdraw ETH2 from the beacon chain. It has modalities that once ETH1 is deposited and burned, Beacon Chain validators then issue ETH2 to the depositors.

Phase 1

Shard Chains: Shard chains are the secret to achieving one of Ethereum 2.0's major breakthrough which is scalability. They are the key to future scalability as they give room for parallel transaction throughput. The main objective of Phase 1 is the "construction, validity, and consensus on the data of these shard chains."

Phase 2

State Execution: This phase is where there will be a transition of shard chains to structured chains and a reintroduction of smart contracts.

Economics

In determining how many validators the network requires to keep the shards going, there are a number of factors to consider. The minimum recommended validators per committee is 111. With 1024 shards the validators will equal 113,664 validators and total ETH will equal 3,637,248. If we would want crosslinks on all shards within a single epoch, the committee size would be 256. That is equal to 8,388,608 total ETH at stake on the network. There's nothing wrong if we have, it simply means crosslinks become rarer.

Staking Rewards

This is a form of incentive for holders of ETH to stake in the network. So, as to encourage those that own ETH to stake in the network, there must be some type of reward.

Without reward, the likelihood that many people would stake their ETH is very low. Serenity boosts the chances of ETH holder staking to the network by paying validators a reward for every block they successfully propose and attest.

This reward system is a scale based on total network stake. Hence, if total ETH stake is low, the issuance rate goes up and as stake rises, it starts to fall. Currently, under the suggested payouts, for every 1,000,000 ETH validating, there is a 181,019 maximum annual issuance, a 0.17% of maximum annual network issuance and an 18.10% maximum annual return rate for validators. It goes differently for other values of ETH Validating; 3,000,000; 10,000,000; 30,000,000 and so on.

Commenting on the stake reward, Vitalik Buterin says "there are a few factors that can decrease issuance in practice to well below those levels:

Validators going offline. Combining the individual and collective penalties, every 1% of validators offline cuts total issuance by around 3%, and if more than 33% ever go offline at once many coins could get burned quickly.

Validators getting slashed. Probably will happen infrequently in practice, but still....

Transaction fees being burned due to EIP 1559 (I estimate ~10k ETH/year initially while usage is still low, ramping up to hopefully hundreds of thousands of ETH/year eventually)

Transaction fees being burned to pay for state rent (this mechanism could possibly be folded into the gas mechanism and hence the EIP 1559 burn)."

Staking Costs

Validating and earning rewards does not come without its costs and attendant risks. A user must consider all these before deciding to become a validator. Some of these costs and risks include;

Capital Acquisition and Lockup Challenges: a user seeking to become a validator must acquire the necessary initial 32 ETH either via purchase or mining. However, stakers can't directly sell staked ETH while it's staked.

In the same vein, to withdraw funds, there is a set amount of time they must wait to get their ETH back. Even though, this time has come down considerably in the latest versions of the spec, the minimum withdraw queue wait is still a whopping 18 hours. There could be a further surge if a lot more people are exiting at the same time but 18 hours will likely be the norm for now.

Computing Cost: a validator will need to run validators clients at a minimum and likely a beacon node as well. This requires computing resources which are quite costly. A beacon node is estimated at $120/year while a validator client is $60/year per validator client.

Code Risk: In staking, there are a certain code risks that users must be wary of involved. This is usually a concern at the very early stages, it becomes less of a concern over time.

The risk as regards code is of two different sides; i.e. the client-side code risk and consensus code risk. In the event of a consensus code break, the network will hard fork and fix it itself. Hence, making it less of a concern. On the flipside, the client-side code risk is a bigger concern because as it'll be hard to decipher whether it is a code break or a malicious fault.

General uptime and maintenance cost -: validators need to be ensured not to experience downtime or they risk a geometric leak on their stake.

For a user with multiple validators, he has to deal with more maintenance cost and worry of the infrastructure.

Security Risk

Apart from possible failures in the client code, stakers hold the responsibility for the security of the environment of their validator clients (internet connection, operating system, hardware, etc.). In the event that their validator client gets hacked due to a security failure, leading to forced downtime and/or misbehavior, there's currently no way to recover funds. This risk is similar to the risk of getting Ether stolen from a wallet due to a hacked laptop or smartphone.

Migration
Migration form Ethereum 1.0 to Ethereum 2.0 involves two major considerations. First, the need to migrate the existing ether must be considered (Ether migration) and secondly, we have to consider transitioning the state of the chain (state migration).

Ether Migration: The idea on ground is that in Phase 0, users on the ETH 1.0 chain will be able to lock up their ether in a contract and will receive an amount of credit equivalent to that locked up ether in ETH 2.0.

There is a debate on the pros and cons of creating either a two-way bridge or one-way bridge between the 1.0 and 2.0 chains. A one-way bridge has major pros of steady security, comparatively lesser complexity and isolation forks to each chain. While a two-way bridge supporters mentions its lower risk of lockup, ability to bring coins back, etc.

State Migration: The most plausible idea is that in phase 2, the state of the current ETH1.0 will be transferred into a shard on the Eth 2.0 chain, and by doing so, all information from the Eth 1.0 chain will be available on the ETH 2.0 chain.

Finally, migration might also see to a replacement of Ethereum Virtual machine (EVM) with eWASM. First proposed in EIP 48, eWASM is a deterministic smart contract execution engine built on the modern standard web assembly virtual machine.

References

https://medium.com/@contentworks/a-brief-history-of-ethereum-3937945d701

https://www.forbes.com/sites/bernardmarr/2018/02/02/blockchain-a-very-short-history-of-ethereum-everyone-should-read/#13f137ea1e89

https://en.wikipedia.org/wiki/Ethereum#History

https://www.blockstuffs.com/blog/history-of-ethereum-from-beginning

https://www.ethereum.org/learn/#ethereum-basics

https://www.investopedia.com/tech/what-dao/

https://www.coindesk.com/ethereums-istanbul-upgrade-arrives-early-causes-testnet-split

https://eips.ethereum.org/EIPS/eip-1283

https://medium.com/nuo-news/istanbul-hard-fork-everything-you-need-to-know-about-it-3a29738934c5

https://ethereumclassic.org/assets/ETC_Declaration_of_Independence.pdf

https://www.coindesk.com/information/what-is-ethereum

https://www.coindesk.com/devcon-shows-ethereums-world-computer-is-a-movement-not-a-product

https://docs.ethhub.io/ethereum-roadmap/ethereum-2.0/eth-2.0-economics/

https://medium.com/ethhub/the-basics-of-ethereum-2-0-economics-3bd2ffe7fd0e

https://docs.ethhub.io/ethereum-basics/what-is-ether/

https://www.cryptimi.com/cryptocurrency-exchanges/cex-io-review#fees

https://bitcoinmagazine.com/guides/what-ether

https://www.coindesk.com/information/what-is-ether-ethereum-cryptocurrency

https://certifikater.vontobel.com/DK/EN/Blog/ether-explained-chapter-2-facts-and-figures-about-ethereum

https://en.wikipedia.org/wiki/Nick_Szabo

https://hackernoon.com/smart-contracts-part-2-the-legality-761cc4bc100d

https://www.coindesk.com/information/ethereum-smart-contracts-work

https://www.ethereum.org/

https://consensys.net/enterprise-ethereum/use-cases/

https://media.consensys.net/40-ethereum-apps-you-can-use-right-now-d643333769f7

https://www.coindesk.com/information/what-is-ethereum